# The City of Refuge Changed Our Lives

## Stories To Inspire You To Take Refuge In God

### Dr Patrick Businge

Copyright © 2018 Dr Ira Roach III

All rights reserved. No part of this publication may be reproduced, distributed, or transmitted in any form or by any means, including photocopying, recording, or any other electronic or mechanical methods, without the prior written permission of the publisher, except in the case of brief quotations embodied in critical reviews and certain other noncommercial uses permitted by copyright law. For permission, write to the publisher at the address below:

Greatness University Publishers
info@greatness-university.com
www.greatness-university.com

ISBN: 978-1-9993481-1-3
ISBN-13: 978-1-9993481-1-3

# DEDICATION

To everyone that has ever felt like church will not solve any of the problems that you face.

To every person that has suffered hurt at the hands of a person or people you love.

To everyone who has ever felt like a misfit and that you do not belong on earth.

To the young person that feels as though they have no voice and that nobody is listening.

# CONTENTS

|    | Endorsement | v |
|----|---|---|
|    | Foreword | 1 |
|    | Introduction | 5 |
| 1  | Awaken My Identity | 9 |
| 2  | Beloved Community | 17 |
| 3  | Becoming One Under God | 23 |
| 4  | Called to Prophesy | 29 |
| 5  | Discover My Gifts | 35 |
| 6  | Filtered Purpose | 43 |
| 7  | Freedom To Be Victorious | 51 |
| 8  | From Addiction To Dedication | 59 |
| 9  | From Broken To Breakthrough | 69 |
| 10 | From Comfort Zone To Growth Zone | 79 |
| 11 | From Lost Boy to Beloved Husband | 89 |
| 12 | Overcoming Emotional Abuse | 97 |
|    | About the Author | 107 |

# The City of Refuge Changed Our Lives

# CONTENTS BY CO-AUTHOR

| 1 | Andre Hudson Jr | 9 |
| 2 | Anika Stewart | 59 |
| 3 | Candie Quick | 79 |
| 4 | Joshua & Cecil Smith | 23 |
| 5 | David Smith | 29 |
| 6 | Dr. Darrell M. Canady | 97 |
| 7 | Dr. Ira Roach III | 9 |
| 8 | Gordon Walker | 43 |
| 9 | Hanan N Major | 69 |
| 10 | Isaiah M Kilgo-Felder | 89 |
| 11 | Martina Jackson | 17 |
| 12 | Myrtice Julius | 51 |
| 13 | Stephon Davis | 35 |

# The City of Refuge Changed Our Lives

The City of Refuge Changed Our Lives

# ENDORSEMENT

Dr Patrick Businge
Founder of Greatness University

# The City of Refuge Changed Our Lives

# ENDROSEMENT

We live in a world characterised by poverty, plagued by the shortage of hope, and marred with average performance. In the midst of this world, the City of Refuge has not remained a spectator. Under the leadership of Dr Ira Roach III, it has embarked on the mission of preaching the Word of God and living the Gospel values.

It is with immense pleasure and immeasurable joy that I present to you **The City of Refuge Changed Our Lives**. In this book, you are going to read stories from people whose lives have been transformed by The City of Refuge. At the heart of these stories are men and women who continue to live ordinary lives in extraordinary ways. Read and discover these real life stories told from the heart to inspire you to respond to take refuge in God.

Dr Patrick Businge
Founder of Greatness University

# The City of Refuge Changed Our Lives

# ACKNOWLEDGMENTS BY DR IRA ROACH III

To the person who birthed this ministry with me, I appreciate all that you have done and it is apparent that the tools you have given the people and me, are still be utilized to empower and bring change.

To my uncle, Bishop Frank Roach Sr., thank you for being the Christian man that I marked. Your life exemplified that of a powerful, anointed and wisdom filled mentor. Thanks for the lessons you taught me as a young boy in life, personally as a saved young person and in Sunday School.

To Bishop Marvin L. Morris Sr., thank you for pulling me to the side at age nineteen and telling me that you believed in me when a lot of people were breathing negativity about my character.

Last but not least, To Bishop Mary L. Alexander (Late Austin Alexander) for loving me back to life. Thank you for birthing me into ministry and allowing me to realize that God did have a purpose for me on this earth.

# The City of Refuge Changed Our Lives

# FOREWORD

**Dr Ira Roach III**
**Senior Pastor**

# The City of Refuge Changed Our Lives

The City of Refuge Changed Our Lives

# FOREWORD BY DR IRA ROACH III

I remember battling with depression from a very early age; and even worse, I didn't want to live on the earth anymore. I hated who I was and did not understand why God even allowed me to be born. You may ask why did someone so young have such a dismissal outlook on life? The constant bullying from school, the put downs from family and the judgement from the church caused me to create the ugly perception of myself.

Never did I even have a feeling like I would ever be used by God to help people in any form of ministry. I found myself very unconfident, with a low self - perception and shy to be in front of people. Although my mind said "everyone will talk about you", I still could always tell people who needed help. I could "feel" them sort of and I would pray for them, especially young people who were sad. I promised myself that if I ever got the chance to make people happy, I would give it my very best shot! I wanted to see people happy and to live a good life!

When I was about 10, I watched Rocky II. At the end of the movie when he was declared the winner, I wasn't cheering but I was crying! My dad said, "Dummy, why are you crying, he won?" I answered, "Because his wife is happy and now they can still be

## The City of Refuge Changed Our Lives

married!" At this point in time, I knew then that I had something unique inside of me and my passion was to see people happy. I was finally directed to a ministry that would love me unconditionally and birth me into the awesome individual that God has blessed to be a blessing to so many people.

July 2019 will mark 15 years that this ministry has been standing, not perfect but it is the perfect church for imperfect people. I pray that these stories will inspire you to seek higher than your friends, family and even your worst fears. God is awesome and just as he has helped many souls at the City, there is somewhere he can help you transform your life through him. Please be transformed and do not ever be conformed to this world! I love you and God loves you more!

Senior Pastor- Apostle Dr Ira D. Roach III

The City of Refuge Changed Our Lives

# INTRODUCTION

# The City of Refuge Changed Our Lives

# The City of Refuge

The City of Refuge Church Inc. was established in July of 2004 and began as the "House of Refuge". In 2006, the Lord spoke to Pastor Roach and told him that the name of the church had to change due to the great vision that God had in his belly. After months of praying, the name was changed from "House of Refuge" to "City of Refuge"! Throughout the years, many hardships and trials came against the ministry, but God still allowed us to stand. There is a scripture reference that has been established for our ministry and the vision that God has given the leader. It is from 1 Samuel 22:1-2:

> So David departed from there and escaped to the cave of Adullam; and when his brothers and all his father's house heard about it, they went down there to him. ²Everyone who was suffering hardship, and everyone who was in debt, and everyone who was discontented gathered to him; and he became captain over them. There were about four hundred men with him.

We built this mission statement from the scriptures:

## The City of Refuge Changed Our Lives

> "Helping people recover from hurts, habits, and hang-ups in order to positively impact themselves, their families, and their communities."
>
> #theCITY

This is the core mission of our ministry and in our book the following stories that you read will present people who once were "fed-up, broke and in trouble," and met God through the City of Refuge. We pray that these stories will encourage, uplift and reestablish your faith in God.

The City of Refuge Changed Our Lives

# Awaken My Identity
# Andre Hudson Jr

Author of 'From Tip to Tails'

# The City of Refuge Changed Our Lives

The City of Refuge Changed Our Lives

# Awaken My Identity

Andre "Demetrius" Hudson Jr is a Certified Dog Training Instructor, Author and Founder of Dog Gone Good Training Grounds LLC. Andre's goals are to help implement dog training tools and knowledge to help modify dog training behaviors. Andre's career began in April of 2014 where he became a Dog Trainer at Petco in Seaford Delaware and was employed there for 2 years.

Andre's entrepreneurial lifestyle began in 2016 when he established Dog Gone Good Training Grounds LLC where he offers obedience training, service dog training, therapy dog training, protection training and show training. Andre has published his 1st book called "From Tip to Tails" revolving around his dog training career. Andre's favorite quote by Charles R. Swindoll is, " Life is 10% of what happens to you and 90% of how you react to it". Here is his story on how The City of Refuge changed his life.

My journey began in October of 2016 when I attended my friend Gordon S Walker Jr's birthday service. Apostle Roach III had pulled me out that Saturday morning and said, "you need to open your mouth" as he put blessing oil on my mouth. I came from a church where I had all these gifts, talents and abilities but they were smothered and weighed down by the things that were suppressing me. After hearing Dr Roach saying those words and talking with me in a room along with two other leaders and

## The City of Refuge Changed Our Lives

my friend Gordon S Walker Jr, it opened my eyes on where I needed to attend.

I came to the City of Refuge Church Inc at the age of 23. I came broken down with hurts, habits and hang ups such as: molestation and rape, affirmation and validation issues, daddy and emotional issues, depression and identity crisis. When I came to The City of Refuge, I remembered their mission which was: To help people recover from their hurts, habits and hang ups in order to positively impact themselves, their families and their communities. Receiving their love, prayers, and praise is what captivated me into staying at The City of Refuge.

Sitting in the church in Milford is where it all began, I was asked to preach on a platform service with a few others on the topic of "I am a King". I accepted and said yes that I would preach on the platform service. I got there last and preached on the topic "God's Not Through with Me Just Yet" and the subtopic "There's Life Still In Me". After preaching the message and the praise filling the room of the church, Apostle Roach called me to the front of the church and anointed me with oil. He was pouring into me those things that I was needing at that time. He then spoke into my life that my path would lead me to one day be Youth Pastor of the City of Refuge Church Inc.

When I heard him VALIDATE me and AFFIRM me as this "PASTOR", it was something that I was seeking. Remember I was growing up in a fatherless

## The City of Refuge Changed Our Lives

home and a single mother raising me was nothing but validation into which made me feel like I was somebody. Given that Apostle Roach validated me and affirmed me, it gave me the hope that I am somebody in the church because of things that were said to me prior.

The City of Refuge showed so much love to me as I was attending all their services. To see so many young people wanting to praise God grasped my attention within the ministry. To hear these great leaders preaching and teaching helped ease my mind throughout my entire transition into the church. Apostle Roach and I had a one on one at his school. We talked about ministry and my personal life which encouraged me because I did not have anyone that I really could talk to. At that point and time in my life, I was missing my father who was never in my life and never showed up for none of my youthful activities or graduations.

I had a void that needed to be filled because it was hard seeing other boys with their fathers and me not having one at all. This is when I began calling Apostle Roach "DAD" because of what I saw in him and what I was looking for all along. Growing within The City of Refuge, Apostle Roach began to teach on "IDENTITY CRISIS "and knowing WHO YOU ARE! These teachings were what I needed because when I transitioned into The City, I did not know who I was at all. All I know was that I was broken down, fatherless, no good, unemployed, would not "mount" to anything, going to be like your father, another statistic, and drug addict. As I continued my journey with The City, Dr. Roach always said "Boy, you better know who you are… Don't be nobody else but yourself."

I struggled trying to find out who I was. Identity crisis was a big factor in my life when I came to the city. During the process of me getting to know who I was, I had to let some things go and be free to understand my purpose and who I was. As time went by, I began to do things that I was never comfortable doing such as starting my own business, networking with other people, going to lots of functions, hanging out with some of the workers, and building relationships with them.

With the help of Apostle Roach and The City of Refuge, I end up becoming a great man that now knows who he is. The City of Refuge helped push me into being free from my molestation and rape, getting free from depression, and more. The City of Refuge is a place of peace, a hospital, and an advocacy center for broken people. If I had not came to the City of Refuge, then I would not be able to write my story out for you all today. The City helped me, danced with me, chastised me, rebuked and corrected me but it was all out of love and for the bettering of me.

The City helped me in so many ways that I cannot thank them enough for the love and support that they have shown me throughout my entire journey

## The City of Refuge Changed Our Lives

as I progress in ministry. Now being here in the ministry for 3 years has helped make me who I am today. With the help of The City, I know who I am. I have created and established a business, and I work in ministry as a minister and leader. There are so many things that I can say to you all to help you get unstuck from those things that held you bound.

One we must FIND OUT WHO WE ARE. We must build a RELATIONSHIP with God and get to know him. We need to communicate with him, serve him, and love him. Another way to get unstuck and be transformed is to ACCEPT CHANGE. We must be willing to accept change and want to change. Lastly, we need to TAKE RESPONSIBILITY with whatever comes our way. We need to learn to accept what we have done so that we do not make the same mistakes again.

The City of Refuge Church Inc is a ministry based on love, prayer and praise. With The City helping me understand who I am and knowing where I am heading to in life, it gave me hope and peace. If it was not for the City of Refuge, I would not have Dog Gone Good Training Grounds LLC. I would not be an author or a minister of the Lord's church. WELCOME TO THE CITY OF REFUGE.

# The City of Refuge Changed Our Lives

The City of Refuge Changed Our Lives

# Beloved Community
# Martina Jackson

Evangelist, author and Speaker

# The City of Refuge Changed Our Lives

The City of Refuge Changed Our Lives

# Beloved Community

It was Wednesday the year was 2013. There were a few questions I had on the altar that I needed God to answer. I had this overwhelming feeling to move back to Delaware where I lived as a young child. I called a "Fast" to focus solely on Jesus and remove the clutter from my mind. I wanted to make sure this "feeling" was from God! That evening at Bible Study, Bishop Walker spoke into my life. He said if God is telling you to move to another city then move. He continued on to say, God would work out my living situation.

After service I spoke to Bishop about the confirmation I received through the word of God, the delivery of his message, and I also mentioned my fast. At that moment, I knew my time was up in Nashville. I honestly admitted my hesitations about a new church covering. Locating a church home in a new city almost 800 miles away, was the only thing keeping me in Nashville. I was not your typical church girl. I was new to the church thing. I had just given my life to Christ a few months prior. Therefore, finding a church home that was capable of nurturing my gifts and helping me grow was a determining factor of when I would leave. I had a hunger and thirst for God's word and I did not want to lose. Bishop Walker told me not to worry about finding a church home. He said, "God will plant your feet and you will grow." I was at peace, it was important for me to have that reassurance from my leader.

Obedience is better than sacrifice, and I had done both. I moved to Nashville and immediately started writing in my prayer journal prayers to God about my desire to see and experience His miracles, signs and wonders. I had this longing to hear God and know Him on a real intimate level. The night before Thanksgiving was the very first time God spoke to me and told me that I was pregnant with twins. He told me I was going to give birth to a boy and a girl. Imagine God saying something that extreme to you! Breathtaking huh?

Well a battle most definitely developed in my mind. Was this God? Why would he tell me this? (I read this kind of stuff in the Bible however, I never pictured this as a modern day scenario). I went back to my prayer journal and remembered what I asked God for. Since God began to manifest Himself I needed instruction on how to nurture what God was showing and telling me. The church I was currently attending was unable to provide those answers. I began searching for a new church home trusting and believing in what God promised me in 2013, through Bishop Walker, in Nashville.

My first time attending The City of Refuge was in January of 2015. I was having a conversation with Candie Quick, who was already a member of the church, about what God had told me. We were friends and attended the same college together. Very early on in our dealings, I realized her Apostle (Apostle Roach) was the guest preacher of a youth service my former church had hosted. I had never experienced such a powerful move of God in a church service. Actually, I was more intrigued; I had never seen God use someone in such an amazing way. I already wanted to visit his church... so that is just what I did.

After praise and worship, Gods presence had fallen and Apostle Roach had the mic. He began speaking what thus said the Lord. He pointed his finger towards me and the first thing out of his mouth to me was "What the Lord has told you about your body is true." "What the devil will do is cause a battle within your mind." Everything he spoke was just confirming everything the Lord had been telling me. Tears just began to fall. Candie began to praise God with a dance because she knew what situation God was speaking to.

I carried that heavy weight from the time God told me in November until that Sabbath service in January. Those chains were broken over my mind after the words Apostle Roach spoke to me. Only a true man of God would be able to confirm in the flesh what God was saying in the spirit. I have not left the City of Refuge since that Sabbath, it has been four great years!!

Since becoming a member of The City of Refuge I have become an Evangelist, author and inspirational speaker! I found who I was at The City. It is not about the titles I carry; it is about the woman I am. I was introduced to the Sabbath and fell in love with the Old Testament stories and teachings. The City is founded on love, prayer and praise. I have never belonged to a church where I felt enough love to consider and address the members as family.

We have been taught despite how we feel, to choose love no matter what, to pray for others before we pray for ourselves and to always give God praise with a thankful and pure heart! The City of Refuge is blessed to have such an intellectual visionary. Our Apostle is a general in God's Army, a giant in the Spirit and a King on Earth. Apostle Roach has stretched me beyond my goals. Everything God placed inside of me when he created me, Apostle Roach has assisted me in cultivating. He has taught me to endure and has always led by example! I would not be the woman I am in God's Kingdom without the wisdom, guidance and instruction from the God within Apostle Roach! If I had remained fearful I would have never been in God's will, I would have never witnessed the faithfulness of God. The City of Refuge is a manifestation of God's promise!

The City of Refuge Changed Our Lives

# Becoming One Under God
# Joshua & Cecil Smith

# The City of Refuge Changed Our Lives

The City of Refuge Changed Our Lives

# Becoming One Under God

For the 8 years we were in a relationship, we brought two beautiful girl in two the world. We held on to the old school morals and traditions of being only with one person. Even though we were very young we had our trials and tribulations as a young couple, but as well as individuals. We finally decide to open a new chapter in our life to become one under God. We no longer wanted to walk in this life with just a civil union. We knew that we needed to become whole, but did not know what it would all entail.

Pastor Gordon Walker Jr. sat down with us and informed us that if we wanted to get married, we would have to complete pre-marital counseling sessions. We agreed to this but still unsure of what this would bring. We were very confident that we were a solid young couple and nothing could come in between us. As time moved forward, we started our counseling and issues started to arise. This brought to light the things we struggled with not just personally but also in our relationship. Pastor Gordon had us complete a love language assessment. In this assessment, we were able to figure out just the simplest things that were our issues.

We then were told to watch a movie called Courageous. This movie opened our eyes to see how in a marriage it is easy to fall out of love or to get side tracked by others when we are not doing the

## The City of Refuge Changed Our Lives

little things for our spouses. The first key was communication. Communication is a necessary in a relationship with anyone. If it was not for Pastor Gordon educating us, we would have never realized our communication was not as strong as we believed. We become one under God on August 23, 2014.

One week prior to our wedding my hair feel out. I had a bold spot on the top of my head. I had been diagnosed with Alopecia Areata. I felt alone and not so beautiful. Our family had gone to The City of Refuge and they prayed over me, then they prayed over my family. Lady Anika then spoke to me and told me everything was going to be okay. For a moment it felt that time had stopped, my emotions had paused, and I knew she was in the spirit. I felt her and it was like nothing I had ever experienced before: Just pureness and grace. I walked out with confidence after the Sabbath.

Then it was our weeding day. Everything that could go wrong in my eyes did. I was running late to my own wedding and the wedding planners were not prepared at all. The only thing I liked at the time was the cross that I had made for us to get married next to. In the movie Courageous, when the couple renewed their vows, they stood by the wooden cross. I wanted to do the same thing for me, it had greater significance. I was overwhelmed completely when my family walked into The City of Refuge. The atmosphere shifted and I felt empowered. Gordon

# The City of Refuge Changed Our Lives

Walker Jr. married us on that day. Lady Anika read scripture and Apostle Roach made sure everything was in order.

The second key in marriage is power. You are the only one who can give power to others. As time went on, we wanted more and more of God. We as a family were being feed with the word and our family was growing. We then became members of The City of Refuge in October 2014. They truly impacted our lives. We became family no matter the struggles, trails, tribulations, good, bad, ups and downs life could bring. The City of Refuge was always there for us.

One Sabbath, Lady Anika had joined us and spoke to me as the wife that I needed to work on myself and be mindful of my words whether I am angry or not understanding. That I needed to work on building myself up as a woman and tackling personal hurts, habits and hang ups. With her help and guidance, I listened. It was not an easy journey but I was the only one who could fix myself. Neither my husband nor my friends or family could repair me or do the work for me. Even through changes of growth and emotional times, the leaders always pulled together to pray over us and made sure we were okay.

Being the husband I held morals that were instilled in me: to work and provide for the family. Anything that happened in the home I as the man of the home needed to fix it. I had a good upbringing and all the men in the family provided for the home. Apostle Roach taught me as the man of the house to look at my own faults. He reminded me that I needed to be better as the man of the home. As well teaching me how to pick my battles in a relationship, he reminded me that every battle is not to be won. That compromising was one of the strongest keys in a marriage. If you want your spouse to do better, you have to make you self-better first. Lastly, the ups and downs through a marriage helped us grow if we can get through it and not to bring others into our marriage.

The Last key in marriage are the 3 core principles: know your identity, know your spouse, and know your purpose. In a marriage, there is no giving up when you take on those vows through sickness and health, for riches or poor. This is a commitment you are taking not only with your spouse but with God. When things are going well you pray . When things are not in your favor you still pray. You hold on fast to the word that God anointed the household when you became one. With God being first in the home, these key points communication, power, and the 3 core principles helped us in our marriage. They continue to help us grow as a couple and live life abundantly.

The City of Refuge Changed Our Lives

# Called to Prophesy
# David Smith

Pastor at Hebrew Apostolic Assembly

# The City of Refuge Changed Our Lives

The City of Refuge Changed Our Lives

# Called to Prophesy

Hello out there! My name is Pastor David Smith. I am currently the Pastor of a successful ministry by the name of Hebrew Apostolic Assembly, located in Dover, Delaware. I was formally a member of The City of Refuge located in Georgetown, Delaware. I joined the church at the age of 16. During that time, I was in a place of confusion, darkness, bitterness, and hatred. Being a teenager can be difficult when you don't fit in and you stand out, you don't dress how others do, you are quiet and normally to yourself. When you are growing up in church, you try to figure out who you are and what your purpose is in ministry.

Growing up in church, I was constantly put down, called out of my name, and mentally abused, but yet used for the gift that was bestowed upon me. The type of church atmosphere that I grew up in, a lot of times it is spoken over our lives what and who we are supposed to be in ministry. But what do you do when the same people who spoke positive things over your life, eventually turn around and put you down, call you out of your name, and mentally abuse you?

Being at City of Refuge helped me get over a lot of those obstacles. Surely, it was not easy. It was very difficult because the place that I was in caused me not to trust people, especially leadership. Being in that difficult place caused me to realize that

# The City of Refuge Changed Our Lives

sometimes it was easier to hold on to the pain that caused me not to trust, because I did not want to face the same pain again.

There were many Sabbaths that I danced and I sang (background), and I sang and I danced. Prayers after prayers, and being told to let it go. Sometimes I thought I was ready to and then there were other times, I just did not want to. I became very comfortable with being angry and bitter and hateful. I did not care if I was mean to people, or if I hated them, or even if I made them feel their smallest self. The saying "hurt people, hurt people" was my very reality at the time. I started church drama, I even almost fought leadership of other churches. The crazy thing is, it did the exact opposite of what I really wanted it to do. No matter how many people I told off, or tried to fight, for some strange reason I gained long-lasting friendships. Something that I NEVER expected, or even wanted to accept at that time. I was so bitter and hateful that it stunted my growth spiritually, but at the time I did not want to hear any of that.

You hear people say they love you all the time and they are there for you through it all, but I did not experience the actions of that until I got to City of Refuge. I mean after all they did all they could to put up with how I was and still love me the same. So eventually, I gave in, I gave up, I threw in the towel, and I waved the white flag. I eventually began my journey to a place of healing, a place of forgiveness,

# The City of Refuge Changed Our Lives

a place of peace, and a place of confidence. Being at City of Refuge I learned a lot about "myself". I learned about self-love, I learned that I owed it to myself to be a better me. The City of Refuge taught me that if I really wanted anything in life that I had to want if for myself first. My salvation, my peace, my love, my joy, my healing, a positive mentality, I had to want it all for myself.

A lot of times as teenagers, we feel it is necessary to do things for our parents and for our families. Get good grades, graduate high school, go to college, all to make other people feel about us how we should feel about ourselves. The City of Refuge taught me that I have to do what is necessary for me to be my best self without the validations of others. Out of all of these wonderful things that I learned at The City of Refuge, one of the many things that got me through my dark place was it gave me confidence in my gift to sing.

Of course, growing up, I did plenty of solos, I sang background for praise and worship teams, I led songs during praise and worship, I sang in choirs but it was at The City of Refuge where I was pushed into leadership of praise and worship and where I gained confidence in my gift of singing. I did not rush into this at all. I slowly walked into it, but it was Bishop Roach (at that time), that pushed me and encouraged me. When I thought I could not do it, when I thought I was not good enough, it was Bishop Roach who helped me get to that place of I know I can do it, and I know that I am good enough. I have been leading praise and worship from that point on.

Eventually that one push catapulted me into learning that singing was not my only gift. I went from singing to exhorting and from exhorting to flowing in my prophetic gift. I had always known that I was born a prophet but it was at The City of Refuge that I learned how to flow in my gift. So now, I have gained more confidence than I ever expected. Today, not only has my prophetic gift grown for me to speak what Yahweh says but it has given me an ear to hear songs that prophetically speak into people's lives. These songs have allowed me to be able to eventually record, which will be coming soon, and not just touch lives here, but touch lives everywhere.

The City of Refuge Changed Our Lives

# Discover My Gifts
# Stephon Davis

# The City of Refuge Changed Our Lives

The City of Refuge Changed Our Lives

# Discover My Gifts

I have been a part of the city for about 11 years. Since I have been there, my life has changed drastically. When I first became a member of The City of Refuge, I was a timid teenager who found it hard to open up and communicate with others. I had bad trust issues and did not know who I was. I had very little confidence as well. I had little to no knowledge to who God really was.

The first way The City of Refuge changed my life was teaching me to be more open. I was taught to be more open with people. I now know that everyone is not out to hurt me and that there are good people in the world. I know that I can trust others and they will be opened to getting to know and love me for who I am. I am not completely closed to meeting new people and I give many chances today. By me being closed off to meeting people, I kind of hid some of my gifts from the world. I believe this was due to lack of confidence. When you hear people tell you how you are not good enough to do this or that, you will never be this person, or you cannot and never will do this, it starts having you really believe it.

I had so many gifts, talents and so many dreams at a young age but I did not believe they were possible because of those around me. They did not believe in me and did not push me to pursue my dreams. This

all changed once I came to the City. The City pushed me to do things that I would not do normally such as speaking in front of huge crowds or sing.
One of my favorite things to do is sing. The City pushed me to use that gift. It all started with someone hearing me sing in the shower, and that someone told Apostle Roach about it. He then put me on the worship team. At first you could barely hear me sing in church services because of the lack of confidence. There were times where I did not even want to sing. I just did not believe I was good enough, but he would not let me give up. He knew this was something I loved and was great at.

Though I did not see my greatness, he did. After so much pushing, the confidence started to grow. I started to take vocal lessons to make my craft greater. I sung at my college graduation. I even won some talent shows at my school and in the community. The City of Refuge has supported me with all the events. I even auditioned for television shows like The Voice and American Idol. Even though I didn't make the shows, I still keep pushing because he won't allow me to give up. Before I even thought about auditioning for any show, my Apostle would always call me by the name American Idol. He really believes in me musically and vocally.

My confidence is better than it ever was. Not only was confidence gained with just singing, but it was built in so many other ways. I finally have the confidence to speak to people. Going through

## The City of Refuge Changed Our Lives

college, I was prepared for oral presentations and group projects. I became more confident going to job interviews and meeting new people. I believe in myself more than when I first became a member at the City.

The City of Refuge is part of the market place, so we are taught to go after the careers we want to pursue. We are taught not to settle for just the entry level jobs but to work towards our own businesses and getting an education. The City is not just the church where you hear God this and God that, but we are taught how to be real men and women of God. God never wanted us to struggle and be poor. He wants us to go after everything that we deserve and that would give us a better life. The City is where I realized the true meaning of faith without work is dead and work without faith is dead. Instead of waiting, which I probably would have done or at least procrastinated, I have been taught to go after what I want and let God move while I do what I need to do as well. I have graduated from college and now I have a supervisor's job: something I thought would never happen.

I was not always a well behaved child especially when angered but Apostle Roach helped me with my anger problems. I remember getting arrested for a situation I had with someone and he and others from The City of Refuge were right there by my side. They supported me when I was going through the court process and even after that. Things were not

## The City of Refuge Changed Our Lives

always great with my real dad. Someone from The City mentored me and kept me under their wing. They both, my mentor and Apostle, helped me to learn to forgive my dad and encouraged me to build a better relationship with him. There were plenty of church services that Apostle prayed for me and ministered to me about dealing with anger, and we also had our one on ones. Not only did he help me through that but also with a death of my best friend. He also helped me with getting over a significant other, and that's a whole story in itself, ha-ha. He stood with me through those moments even when I was being hardheaded and wanted to do things my own way. He never gives up on people even when he should, that's what I love about him.

One last thing the City helped me with was growing my own relationship with God and trusting in God's Word. Apostle Roach always kept us ready to fight with God's word in our day to day lives. "Depression hits you, use the Word, if you feel discouraged, use the Word", and so on. We were taught how to properly read the Bible and apply it to our lives. He also gets us ready to minister to people we are destined to minister to by giving us the opportunity to first teach The City ourselves. By doing this, he made sure we were ready to be released to teach the word of God to the world outside of The City of Refuge. Apostle Roach taught me how to pray and to use my spiritual gifts.

## The City of Refuge Changed Our Lives

In conclusion, The City of Refuge has always played a big part in changing my life and as a matter of fact changing my world. The City taught me everything from being more open to others, being more confident, letting go of things that hinder growth, going after my dreams, and having a closer walk with God. If you ever feel like you need a change in your life, whether a change in the people you surround yourself with or growing a closer relationship with God or just a better life period, I recommend trying The City of Refuge. Thanks for reading my story of how the City of Refuge changed my life.

# The City of Refuge Changed Our Lives

# Filtered Purpose
# Gordon Walker

# The City of Refuge Changed Our Lives

The City of Refuge Changed Our Lives

# Filtered Purpose

Greetings, my name is Gordon S Walker Jr and this is my story on how City of Refuge Church Inc saved my life. It was in the summer time that City of Refuge Church Inc was mentioned to me by my brother Damien. At that time I was employed at Roses and he asked me to come and hear him preach that Saturday. Here I am saying to myself, "I have to catch my flight." Now anyone who knows my ways understands that I will set aside my plans to go to your event, especially family. My brother did not know I was going to try out to become an adult entertainer. He also knew that I did not like church.

So without telling Damien my plan, I agreed to hear him preach. The one thing I told him was, "No one better not touch me." His response was "Ok, Ok Scott, so are you coming or not?" I said, "Yes, just don't have anyone touch me or I won't come back or I may say something." He boasted about his Pastor and Co-Pastor Roach with confidence about how anointed they were and how the people there entreated him with love. I completely had no interest in this due to the fact he was not talking anything I loved to hear about. Who would have thought that once I accepted to visit the City of Refuge it would change my life and become my place of residence.

So Saturday had come, in which I wore my FUBU red shorts, white T-Shirt, and my black, red and white SHAQS. Once we arrived to the City of

## The City of Refuge Changed Our Lives

Refuge, getting out of the door was different. As we were walking in, the greetings were phenomenal. Even though I had my guard up, I knew how to be polite when someone spoke to me. However, my guard got penetrated because these people were genuine. Damien wanted me to sit in the front row when he preached. That was the first time I heard of a platform service. Moving on, I decided to sit in the back because I was uncomfortable sitting alongside them. He caught a conniption but that was his problem, not mine.

Service began and his praise and worship team that consisted of David Smith, Co-pastor Roach, Elder Carla Morton and Stephon Davis. They sung these songs I had never heard before and did a dance called the wu-tang. The City of Refuge service was vibrant, youthful, upbeat, and full of life. As I observed the environment I was in, I saw nothing but youth and young adults enjoying themselves as they gave praise to God. Looking back at my former ministries, this ministry totally rocked compared to where me and my brother came from.

After the praise and worship, the exhortation that came from one of the young adults was amazing and the shouting that took place with everyone was very interesting to see. To see these young kids play the instruments and the skills these kids had was very motivating for me to want to play the drums again. After each individual on the platform was done, this short black man hops up to give his remarks about

## The City of Refuge Changed Our Lives

what was preached and his passion towards the word had connected with my heart. Because of my past issues with males and me being in a fatherless home, there was no reason for me to even find a male to look up to or listen to.

Surprisingly, this guy named Pastor Roach III caught my four eyes. Not only did he catch my eye but he called me up to the pulpit. He instructed my brother to stand alongside while he spoke to me. So he began to prophesy to and speak into me, my life, and tell me my future through, of course, the Holy Spirit. It was the fact this man was so in tune with the spirit of the living God that he said, "I am not going to touch you because the Holy Spirit told me not to. So, I am going to speak over your life."

Man the feeling that ran through my body got me crying. You could hear the people giving thanks to God for me. The next thing you know I am giving God a dance with the rest of the people. Next week, back to Roses checking out customers. I actually see my favorite adult entertainer where we converse and shares with me they found Jesus the Christ. That moment changed my mind of what I wanted to do.

Really, it was the fact that this short man actually said somethings concerning my life and spoke into my life that it actually brought about a redirection in my purpose. From there on, my life has never been the same again. A few months later, I joined The City of Refuge. You see, with the help of the City, and teaching me to have my own relationship with

God, they tarried with me as my course of direction changed.

I was molested and raped from ages 3-12. All I knew was sex and how to make people feel good to the point my mind was trained that was all I could do. I remember the times where my family encouraged me but it was not as much as I heard how good in bed I was. To me, my family was foreign to me because of the isolation I put myself in. I was having sex multiples times a day including school hours. I had other aspirations yet I practiced one and that one even brought in revenue at times.

My purpose of life had been tainted when I was young and when I got old enough, that was all I knew. So the City of Refuge, for years, worked with me, chastised me with love, and danced with when I was so depressed and suicidal about life. The one thing my leaders and the Roachites (the other workers) encouraged me to do was to change my mind. Get in the word of God to strengthen your mind and know who you are. This was a repetitive speech day in and out and it changed my life.

## Advice zone

My encouragement to you is to really **renew your mind daily.** Once you do that have some boldness to speak up about some things and change your environment and your own thoughts. Next you will find yourself having to **encourage yourself.** I say this because you are used to being around. You have

## The City of Refuge Changed Our Lives

a habit and behavior that needs to be broken. So you will have times of intervention where you are actually withdrawing from yourself (old wineskin) to receive the new (wineskin) you. This is going to self-belief and a strong support system. With the City of Refuge being there, it frustrated me at times but I had to converse with myself and get myself together. It gets serious when you detox yourself and find out the many thought patterns you have, but I got through it.

After you go the rubber-band effect from going through the process, you can start a new chapter of a **Filtered Purpose.** Because the The City of Refuge helped me with this, I have walked into doors that I have not thought I was worthy to be in. It is because of the City of Refuge that I was able to go back to school and complete my education. I now have my own business. The City has taught me well enough on the importance of communication, manhood, my words and how to use them, grooming, and the list can go on. I am literally alive because of the pure blood (life) that runs through the core vein of the City of Refuge.

# The City of Refuge Changed Our Lives

The City of Refuge Changed Our Lives

# Freedom to be Victorious
# Myrtice Julius

## Founder of Revive Ministries Non-Profit Religious Organization

# The City of Refuge Changed Our Lives

The City of Refuge Changed Our Lives

# Freedom to be Victorious

Myrtice is the founder of Revive Ministries Non-Profit Religious Organization. It teaches men and women how to develop, nurture, identify and conquer life's challenges and help them rebuild the skills they need to live an abundant life. Here is her story on how The City of Refuge changed her life.

## A broken vessel

I came to The City of Refuge broken to the core. I didn't know if I was coming or going. I come from a family that believed that you keep all your issues to yourself and no one needs to know your business or problems. In effect, I dealt with many issues as a child living in a broken home. Not being able to speak on the problems that I had seen or felt. I was feeling very confused, angry, and had a lot of unanswered questions. As I lived by the saying that what goes on in your house stays in your house, I kept a lot of issues to myself even as I entered my adulthood.

The people that I surrounded myself with did not understand the pain and misunderstanding of life that I was dealing with as they too were dealing with the same problems and issues inwardly. So, help was very rare and the way I saw and dealt with life was dangerous most of the time. Before I came to the realization of where I needed to be, I had lived in abusive relationships especially with the father of my first child. This abuse was verbal, physical, and mentally but he wasn't the only. I have been raped as a teenager because I was searching for love and belonging. I therefore found myself in the wrong place at the wrong time. Often, I was homeless going from house to house with my two children. I was on the edge of committing suicide and having a mental break down as I tried to survive in streets of Philadelphia.

I could not understand why people did not see my pain. Maybe it is because my tears were hidden. However, my wounds were open as I begged to find a source of healing from somewhere. The more I begged the more my wounds became exposed to my world. I became part of a world that I felt like I could not get out of. I was stuck drowning in my sorrows with partying, sex, liquor, and drugs because my mind-set was in a place where I felt like I AM BY MYSELF. I really needed comfort from somewhere and my somewhere was in those things.

When I came to The City of Refuge I found a freedom there that I have neither felt nor experienced since my childhood. At The City, I did not have to be bound in my skin and sink in the thoughts that I had for years. The City of Refuge was the right place that I found at the right time.

## The right place to be

I was looking for security for so long but it was in my face the whole time. That security was called faith but I did not realize it until a year before I got saved. I was the child you see praising God in the corner of almost every church service. This is because I was raised under the COGIC denomination. I knew about prayer, God and faith but my stubbornness caused me to forget and miss my very purpose of why my mother and father instilled those gifts and knowledge in me as a child. I did not know that I would need them as a teenager or an adult.

During tough times in my life, I would get on my knees and pray. I would also read Scripture when no one was watching me. But I never fully embraced my faith because in my mind I was thinking I am doing too much. I would not sit in no one's church and be a hypocrite. So, one day I woke up from a drunken night and realized I needed to be in someone's church because my security was there. But I do not go to everyone's church. I tried to go to a familiar church that my family use to go to. However, I knew it was not there because my past was still living there. I did not feel the security, the peace, the freedom and my heart was not there.

What happened to me next was not expected. I remember I was broken and I was searching for security and love. On this day, one of my closest friends asked me to come to church with him. We both went to the clubs together and I was shocked that he asked me to go to church. I said yes! I had my bottle liquor waiting for me and a fresh pack of cigarettes. So, my thought was that I am just going to support my soul brother. Mysteriously, this was the day I found my faith again. I was in the right place at the right time.

I continued to work on my faith and this gave me strength from the moment I said yes. There are things and issues that tried to distract my process of growth and healing but I knew my faith was very important. My distractions always came from my family, my marriage, my divorce, losing my child in a sense, and me still wanting to belong somewhere. But I realized that if I stayed in the right place at the right time, these distractions will disappear as they were temporary. I realised that they were there to make me stronger, wiser, and stand tall on a solid ground that could not be shaken.

I therefore stayed at The City of Refuge from the day I received that invitation and never turned backed while I was going through all my transitions. My spiritual father Dr Ira Roach III has always told me and showed me when to stand but also when to keep my mouth shut in every transition and storm. He did not just say it me but he showed it. That was something I needed to see knowing that I have seen a lot of hypocrites and people hurt in the church. So, it was not easy for me to trust a person in the church scene. However, when I joined the City of Refuge, I found it to be a family that stayed together, cried together, ate together, prayed together, danced together, and protected each other. My life has never been the same since that day that was the birth of my freedom.

## Victorious

After realizing my faith, I discovered that my understanding was not based on the thought of people or my past. I was able to stand tall on my own understanding where my security, love, faith, and peace was. This was the victorious feeling you get when you know you are free from being stuck in your mind set and not able to see the big picture of where you belong or where you were going. When you felt like your purpose or life was just worthless. All those things you carried for years that no one understood you did not even understand the whys of your own tribulations and storms. However, I was set up for a VICTORIOUS come back that I did not know was coming. Victorious grounds do not shake. There was no more hiding behind a mask. I therefore encourage you to stay in the right place at the right time. You are standing on VICTORIOUS GROUNDS! Your task in this is to find out who you are. Your task is to find out where your faith stands and stay there so that you allow it to grow within you. Do not allow yourself to live in past or be a victim of your past. Find a community that you

## The City of Refuge Changed Our Lives

can trust and know that at the end of the day you are safe and loved by the one who designed you! This is what the City of Refuge became for me: a community of love, peace and hope.

The City of Refuge Changed Our Lives

# From Addiction to Dedication
# Anika Stewart

Author, Life Coach, Inspirational Speaker, and Counselor

# The City of Refuge Changed Our Lives

The City of Refuge Changed Our Lives

# From Addiction to Dedication

Anika Stewart is the founder and CEO of Embracing Your Inner Woman, Author, Life Coach, Inspirational Speaker, Counselor in faith based and Co-occurring disorders, Creator of Self Identity Apparel and Community Activist. She is also the founder of the I'm Every Woman Conference.

Anika is known for her bold, direct and confident approach of compelling women to transform their lives. Women are inspired through her story of overcoming addiction, domestic violence, separation in marriage and single parenting. Anika empowers single women to combat their fear, doubt and self-limits of pursuing their goals. She helps them to release the pain, rediscover who they are and emerge with confidence and clarity, so they can activate their voice, hope and opportunity in their life. Some of the signature talk titles are: I Choose To LIVE, The Power of Your Breakthrough, When You Want to Give up, Give In, and While You Wait.

Today, Anika is the Author of her memoir *Diaries of an Elect Lady* and her self-help book titled *Expose Unveil Discover: The Inner Woman Workbook & Guide*. She has a support group known as Live Outreach Ministry for women to be liberated, improve, be vivacious and enlightened through the transitions of all life's challenges. She understands the emotions of being alone, hopeless and unstable while on this journey; and strives to help others pull through as well. As appreciation for her exemplary attributes, she was honored with the Prestigious Lady of Excellence in Leadership Awards and Empowered Women of the Year for Educational Advancement. Anika is congenial and passionate about the lives she encounters. She is an example to women of all diversities.

Today, in the year of 2018 I am best known for being the Inspirational Speaker, 2x Best Selling Author, Certified Christian Life Coach and Ordained Elder of City of Refuge. I serve my community, clients and workers of The City of Refuge with the intention to impact their lives and disrupt the self-doubt, self-limits and fear that cripples them from moving forward and living out their dreams.

Do you desire more out of life? You are tired of waking up stuck and uncertain of what direction to take! Or how about you know there is more for you but you are not quite sure what to do next! I can actually identify with these feelings all too well. I remember thinking to myself I am not worth living a life of happiness. See I was living this frightful lifestyle of drug addiction, I was using and selling drugs out of my home with my three children at that time.

Understand, at this time in my life I was living in Manchester Square: a neighborhood in the hood of Dover, Delaware where violence, drugs, and poverty

## The City of Refuge Changed Our Lives

was normal. With this in mind, my mother did her best to raise me and my five siblings. I was in church service every Sunday and every revival, but the reality was that our environment was a major influence in my life. I was being taught about Jesus Christ and I loved attending church services, I sang in the choir, and even created a choir in the neighborhood but those days would be short lived as I began to reach the age of rebellion.

Several years later, I was 12 years of age and my life took a turn for the worst. I began to become rebellious and no longer had the desire to attend church. I started acting out in school and in the home by sneaking out the house in the middle of the night, smoking cigarettes and marijuana. What started out as recreational use quickly advanced to daily use that expanded to a drug addiction that would control my lifestyle. My lifestyle became consumed with drugs and all that involves; so the little church girl was no longer a church girl in the neighborhood but now a teenage mother at the age of 14, high school dropout at the age of 16, and 3 children at the age 18 years of age.

My addiction led me to a life of self-destruction and low self-esteem. I lacked self-worth and made bad decisions with prioritizing what was important. I allowed my daughter to witness me self-medicating with alcohol and drugs such as PCP and marijuana. For instance, I found myself grabbing my daughter and running through the same neighborhood I grew up in (Manchester Square) to get away from her father in the middle of the night because he was attempting to beat me. When was it going to be enough? In my mind, I thought this was my life and this was all I was good enough for. I would say to myself, "If he hits me, he loves me and if he calls me out my name, he cares."

I knew there was more to my life than this, but I was so far gone in the lifestyle of fast money and addiction that I became complacent. As a little girl, I was exposed to who God was and heard so many times, "God is going to use you. You have a calling on your life. You are chosen." I knew the power of God's name and witnessed His miracles, healing and deliverance. So then, I became involved in another relationship with a young man. For the love of money, I let this man sell drugs out of my home with my three children. At this point in time, my addiction had advanced. I was abusing alcohol, marijuana, PCP, and Xanax on a daily basis. There were days when I did not know if I was coming or going, but I loved being high and I loved going out to the clubs.

On this particular day, it was sunny and I had been out shopping, getting my hair done, and hanging with my girlfriend. All of a sudden, she gets a knock on her door from the people in the neighborhood exclaiming, "Nika! The cops ran in your house!" The cop put me in handcuffs and escorted me to his vehicle. All of this was done in front of my son. I

## The City of Refuge Changed Our Lives

felt humiliated and frightened and my son was crying for me. I couldn't believe this was happening.

I was sitting in the jail cell alone. As I was crying and scared I prayed, "Father God, in the name of Jesus, I need you to move now. If you move in this situation I will change my ways. I don't want to live this lifestyle no more. God help me and guide me. I don't know what to do no more. I need you Jesus!" Later that night, I was released on bail to my family – not the friends that I hung out with; not the friends I smoked with every day; not the friends that were at my house every day to chill with me. I entered an empty home in disarray. I was depressed and ashamed and couldn't believe I let myself get to this place in my life. Despite me just being released from bond, my family loved on me.

A few weeks went by and I got an invitation to a church service from my baby brother on a Saturday morning. As a result, my life was never the same on May 12, 2007. As the church service was moving along, God used the Bishop to speak a Word in my life. The Bishop confirmed that God was with me and as he spoke, I received the words of life. I decreed unto God, "I shall not die, but live." Then, I gave God my best praise.

I had begun to attend service every week. This experience was different. I was intrigued and enlightened about the knowledge of the Sabbath. For the first time, I understood the Word of God

## The City of Refuge Changed Our Lives

that was being preached and taught through my leaders, Bishop Roach, and his wife at that time. I felt alive and free again but I was still holding on to that man in my life. Although I was holding on to what was comfortable for me, Bishop Roach never judged me. He continued to provide me with counsel, guidance and the word of God. The City of Refuge saved my life because it was a place of safety. I felt harmless in the presence of God and his servant leaders. The leaders helped me identify my gifts and talents and provided the resources demanded to bring me to the next level in my life.

I was delivered from drugs, low self-confidence, depression, guilt, shame, soul ties and fornication. I was able to pursue my purpose and calling in life with the guidance, support and accountability from Apostle Roach and The City of Refuge. Without this ministry being prevalent in my life I would be dead, and my children would be motherless. I am forever grateful!!

I would like to end by sharing with you some tips on how to embrace adversity. The easiest thing to do is give up when you are feeling stressed, overwhelmed, frustrated or depressed. We all have a purpose but the purpose will not be revealed in your life during the time things are going according to plan. Purposes are created and birthed in the moment of adversity. Adversity arises then disrupts your happiness and unsettles you to push you in

## The City of Refuge Changed Our Lives

assignment. Therefore, you must embrace the hardships in your life and use them as tools, life lessons, and opportunity to tell your story of victory.

Change The Mindset/ Perception
- ✓ Ask God what am I to learn from this transition?
- ✓ Focus on the goal not your emotions
- ✓ Encourage someone else (derailing) divert your attention

Position Yourself
- ✓ Pause – take a moment to meditate, be still and be quiet
- ✓ Be in control and rebuild
- ✓ Evaluate and assess the who/what barriers/distractions

Create A Solid Foundation
- ✓ What's worth having is worth fighting for
- ✓ Be willing to sacrifice
- ✓ As you endure you gain maturity/ self-development

Do The Work
- ✓ What situation are you facing in your life presently?
- ✓ What are some possible life lessons and tools you can possess from this hardship?
- ✓ What emotions are causing you to become complacent?
- ✓ Name the distractions (person, place or thing)

Implementation Dialogue

# The City of Refuge Changed Our Lives

- ✓ For the next 21 days, once a day confess openly the emotions that will no longer hold you in captivity while looking at yourself in the mirror.
- ✓ How did it feel as you released those confessions?
- ✓ Write a letter to the distractions and address how they will no longer be a part of your life. Then proceed to burn the letter and witness the elimination.

The City of Refuge Changed Our Lives

# From Broken To Breakthrough
# Hanan N Major

## Founder of Agape Love Transitional Homes

# The City of Refuge Changed Our Lives

The City of Refuge Changed Our Lives

# Agape Love Transitional Homes

Hanan N. Major is the CEO and Founder Agape Love Transitional Homes. Her largest blessings are her 2 biological children, one adopted son, and her husband. She graduated in 2006 with a) Bachelor's Degree in Social Work (BSW). Since 1999, Hanan has been assisting homeless women with children to recovery by providing resources and allowing them to live with her until adequate shelter is located. She's an advocate at heart. She assisted these women with food, clothing, transportation, employment search, resume building, domestic violence assistance, mental health/substance abuse evaluations, child care, and a host of other needs.

Hanan has worked with the youth for over 20 years and understands the dynamics of children with instability and trauma. Her goal has always been to lessen the instability which is a great gateway for traumatic events for the parents and the children. Hanan has 16 years of Case Management experience. She has provided case management services to youth and adults with mental health/substance abuse, domestic violence, housing, educational, social, behavioral, self-care/personal and hygiene issues.

In 2007, Hanan and her children were forced to be homeless (while being married with a home) due to domestic abuse and did not know where to go or what resources were available. They were homeless for 1 year while she had a degree, full-time job, reliable transportation, and childcare. She rented rooms, stayed at places with no running water, no electric, and stayed in an attic while just having 3 mattresses. In 2008, Hanan had had enough and began to talk to people about her situation (she was afraid, unaware of where she could obtain assistance, and embarrassed) and began to receive resources.

Throughout all of the turmoil, Hanan remains a faithful advocate for homelessness in general but has a huge passion for homeless women with children, pregnant homeless women, and homeless women in the reunification process. Her organization provides housing, resources, and trainings for these women and children, in a transitional setting. In 2017, she became a Licensed Insurance Agent for both Delaware and Maryland. She also began writing her autobiography titled "Tainted Love". In 2018, she opened another business that sells scented goods by the name of Scentsy by Hanan Major.

The City of Refuge Changed Our Lives

# From Broken To Breakthrough

Hello my name is Hanan Major. I joined The City of Refuge Church (previously known as The House of Refuge) in 2004. At that time, I had been through hell and back starting at childhood. I was molested from the age of 5-13 by a first cousin. Molested by an uncle-in-law from the age of 5-7. My mother had left me with my grandparents, for them to raise me. I was bullied about hygiene, my clothes, horrible acne, etc. I began a life of fighting and promiscuity at the age of 13. At the age of 16, I was almost charged with attempted murder.

Weeks later, the same man held me at gun point in the middle of a Royal Farms parking lot. At that very point, I could care less whether I lived or died. This life led me to constantly fighting and dating numerous men, one in which raped my 12-year-old sister in our home. I had been abused sexually, physically, mentally, emotionally, and psychologically by men. This led me to seek love from anyone that would give it, including women. All I ever wanted was to be loved. I had 2 children in hopes that it would fill the voids in my life. This kept me busy, but I was torn apart by extreme reoccurring traumatic events in my life.

When I joined the church in 2004, I had my walls of protection up so thick that I thought no one could ever get in. I had recently gotten married and I still didn't trust anyone with lives of my children or

## The City of Refuge Changed Our Lives

myself, not even my husband. I had no self-esteem nor did I have a clue what I was created or why GOD wouldn't just take my life the same as HE gave it. If I didn't have any children, I would have had absolutely no reason to live.

I remember the very first visit to the church like it was yesterday. The Pastor of the church (Pastor Ira Roach III) spoke a word that I know was directly from the mouth of GOD himself. Some of the things that had happened to me were unknown to man and hit me like a ton of bricks when GOD revealed it to the Pastor. I began to come on a regular basis. Then I started going to Bible studies, prayer, watch night etc. This ministry taught me to pray earnestly, the fundamentals of faith, fasting, how to read my Word, and even how to understand the Word from its original manuscripts.

The City of Refuge Church helped me to see a glimpse of myself through the eyesight of God. They helped me understand why I had been through so much. They taught me about the power of healing. As the healing process took place week after week, I began to think, maybe I am someone. Maybe, just maybe, I had a purpose. Those days at the City of Refuge had turned into weeks, the weeks into months, and those months turned into years of me being saved, healed, set free, and delivered.

The anointing of God in "The City" was like no other church that I had ever visited or been a member of. Each time that I would enter the House

## The City of Refuge Changed Our Lives

of GOD, miracles began to happen to me and my children. These miracles began to change me from the inside out. I began to feel like I was worth being created. Through much prayer and supplication, my self-esteem began to rise rapidly. I began to have a sense of self-worth. My identity crisis was coming to an end.

After finding out that I was worth something and realizing that nothing in the past could be changed, moving forward was my only option. The Pastor (now Bishop Ira Roach III) began to meet with me to discuss my future, goals, interests, passions, and desires. He asked me about obtaining a degree. I fought and sexed my way through High School, so I didn't think that I was intelligent enough to go to college never the less, obtain a degree. He helped to obtain a Bachelor's degree in social work. I knew that I loved to help people but had not the first clue as to obtaining a degree in the field that I loved so much to be able to start a career in this area.

After obtaining employment in the Human Services field, the church and the ministry continued to push me towards greatness. The Pastor (now Apostle Ira D Roach III) walked me through the process of obtaining my very own Non-Profit Organization known as Agape Love Transitional Homes. I had been allowing broken, homeless women with and without children to reside with me for years. Apostle Roach showed me a way to not interrupt my home environment while teaching me to continue to do

## The City of Refuge Changed Our Lives

what I was so passionate about, which is helping broken women such as I was to recover, become stable, and heal. Through helping all these women overcome many of the same obstacles and barriers that I had faced my entire life, boosted my self-esteem, morale, self-worthiness, and gave me even more purpose.

I was previously a very timid person with little to no confidence especially with speaking in front of others. With my Non-Profit, I had to begin going to business meetings, sharing my organizational information with the state and other non-profit organizations to solicit for funding. Through this, it helped me to build an uncountable number of professional relationships. While building these relationships, this ensured me of my sense of purpose.

As I was continuing to grow, my husband at the time was very stagnant and hesitant to see me flourish. What I thought was a happily ever after began to turn sour. I tried to encourage his growth as much as I could. He felt like I was now trying to control him, and he wasn't having it. You see, he was 16 years older than I and he began to lose the control over me that I had been too naive to even know existed. This turned into a messy divorce and the verbal, mental, sexual and psychological abuse that I endured caused a relapse in who I thought I'd become. I felt like my accomplishments meant absolutely nothing without a complete family. I ran

## The City of Refuge Changed Our Lives

from everyone and everything that had shown me love and taught me how to be an overcomer through Christ. This only lasted for a short time.

Apostle Ira Roach III and the members of The City of Refuge came to my children and I's rescue. Apostle Ira Roach III counseled me while he and The City of Refuge prayed life back into me. Life went on. Now I can proudly say that I am happily married to the King of my dreams. I host food banks for the less fortunate. I serve whole meals to the community on Thanksgiving and Christmas. I do coat, hat, and mitten drives in the winter months. I partner with the toys for tots and serve over 40 families a year at Christmas time.

I still have my transitional homes where I house homeless women with children. We teach them daily living skills, help with education, work on job readiness skills and help them with credit repair. Apostle Roach has taught The City of Refuge how to be healthy, wealthy, and wise while serving the needs of others and creating residual income. I am a Life Insurance Agent, licensed in Delaware and Maryland. I am the owner of Scentsy by Hanan Major. I am also in the process of finishing my autobiography titled "Tainted Love."

Life has its way of throwing you topsy turvy, but God has His way of showing up and showing out. He will allow the right people to be in your life to pray for you, believe in you, push you, motivate you, encourage you, and remind you who you are through

## The City of Refuge Changed Our Lives

eyesight of God. He has already won the battle for you! If I'm never able to impart into your life again, remember that its ok to be "Broken", just don't allow your brokenness to destroy you. Utilize every experience in life to teach, motivate, encourage, and help someone else overcome what didn't destroy you. God has given us gifts, tools, resources, and people that help us in every way. Use these self-help tools to gain health, wealth, and happiness. Until we meet again, may God ever pour out His blessings, favor, healing, and love upon your lives.

The City of Refuge Changed Our Lives

# From Comfort Zone to Growth Zone
# Candie Quick

Minister at The City of Refuge

# The City of Refuge Changed Our Lives

### The City of Refuge Changed Our Lives

# From Comfort Zone to Growth Zone

Candie Quick works as an Educator with Boys and Girls Club. On a daily basis, she tries to inspire at risk children to follow their dreams and know that they can achieve anything that they put their mind to.

Candie is also the founder and CEO of Quick Designs. She specializes in logo design, branding, and web design. She offers design services to aspiring and emerging entrepreneurs, ultimately taking their ideas and vision to craft creative solutions to their business marketing problems.

Candie has worked diligently with children and finding a way to inspire them through using art to express how they feel. She found a way to combine Quick Designs and her love for children to better the community. Candie received her Associates in the Science of Elementary Education and is currently pursuing her Bachelors degree in Educational Studies. She has been honored to be on the Dean's list, awarded Student of the Block for her service to the school, and Employee of the Month. Here is her story on how The City of Refuge changed her life.

I went to the City back into 2014 with one of my classmates. In 2014, I was on 5-6 mental health medications as I was diagnosed with 5 mental health issues. I was suffering from major depression, generalized anxiety, borderline personality disorder, obsessive compulsive disorder, and post-traumatic stress disorder. I was going to counseling and taking medication since I was eight years old! Counseling and medication was a normal routine in my life.

## From comfort zone

I was a girl that didn't know what it was like to live in the real world. As a child I didn't believe I really existed. My mom was a single mom for most of my early years. Even when she got married, we still struggled for money. My great uncle would send me letters and money throughout the school year. So, every summer and Christmas, my great uncle (who was like a father to me) would come up from West Virginia to see us. My mom would send me to my grandfather's house and every summer my great uncle would touch, kiss, and rape and molest me every other night. He told me that I was his favorite because I didn't fight! I was told that I was ungrateful, and I should feel ashamed about talking like that with everything that he has done for me. This taught me to not speak my truth.

As time went on, my mother kept physically and mentally abusing me. In her mind that is how she loved me. I got older and started to resent her. On Mother's Day Weekend, I went to stay with my biological father. That weekend just proved to me that men could do what they wanted to young girls

## The City of Refuge Changed Our Lives

and no one would believe us. I was given a white pill for a headache, and it made me very drowsy. I remember laying on the floor, asking my father what he was doing over me, and him telling me that "he was just checking on me". As he said that, I felt my pants, and under garments coming off. I couldn't move. My eyes rolled in the back of my head, and I was out again. I woke up with it being Sunday, and I convinced him to take me to church. I tried telling the people that I thought could help me but they didn't think nothing of it. So, I didn't say anything until July when I broke down at camp. This is when my life turned from a painful toleration to I can't take it no more!

With my history of abuse, I tried killing myself but I was unsuccessful. I did a lot of research about dying, killing yourself, and self-mutilation. Self-mutilation was my way of escaping the pain of "I am not going to be anything, but a toy to men, I am not loveable, and my opinions does not matter". I was also told in the church world that if I was to kill myself, then I was going to hell. A place in my mind, I was already there, so what it more torment added to torment. At one point, I was ok with going to hell because at least then, I would have had some control of my outcome.

In all of this, I continued to work, and go to school. I talked to a few more counselors in school and out of school. Medication and more medication was all I received. Even with all the medications, I still was cutting, I still hated myself, and I still wanted a genuine place that I belong too, that I didn't have to do anything, but be myself.

## To the growth zone

My classmate, told me that she normally doesn't invite people to her church but she felt like God told her to take me. She told me to come stay with her at least on the weekends and I could ride to church with her. This is where the City began to change my life. At her house, I met Apostle Roach. I normally don't trust men, nor guys very quickly. However, Apostle Roach was different. To me, he had a spirit that I haven't felt in a long time. He reminded me of my "Uncle Winky". I knew I was safe with him and could possibly get answers to my questions.

We spent hours talking, and me telling him, I still don't understand, and we would go over topics again and again. This started my healing process, because there was a person that actually believed me. It gave me hope, that I could actually overcome, and just maybe stop cutting.

I went to service one Saturday and Apostle Roach was not there. I felt a bit weird because I connected with him. My classmate was there and reassured me that everything was going to be ok. I was still getting used to women preachers. This woman got up there, and began to preach a message called "FREEDOM". She asked me if she could pray for me. Being an adopted church girl, I didn't say no. I

## The City of Refuge Changed Our Lives

really wanted to be free! She told me "Freedom starts in your Mind". I have to choose to be free. This was something that I never heard before. I have the choice to freedom. I had to process this. I didn't go and ask any questions. I didn't talk to anyone from the City that week. I was quiet and asked God to show me what to do.

The next week, I gathered all my medications and handed them to Apostle Roach. He thought it was a bag of candy. In my mind, I thought wow I have enough mediation for people to think its candy, what the heck is wrong with me. I was told by the counselor's I would never be able to survive without medication. I was determined to prove them wrong. Apostle Roach asked me if I was sure that I wanted to do this. He said, "I am not going to have your counselors say that my church made you give up your medication, and you go do something crazy to yourself". I told him I was ready to come off, and he said ok. We agreed that if I felt like I needed them back, then I would call him. He would then meet me and I would get them back. I only called once and he talked me through my mini-crisis. I haven't been on medication since then. Over time, I joined the City of Refuge. At times, Apostle would tell me, "do we need to send you back to the counseling woman?" With tears in my eyes, I would respond "no". I got myself together and figured out how to survive and deal with real life situations.

## Advice Zone

If I could give three points to anyone that has been through abuse, and dealt with mental health, then it would be:

- ✓ You're not alone
- ✓ Know that your voice matters
- ✓ Seek help.

## You are not alone

There are people that can help you when you are in a moment of despair. For me, I sought God! God led me to the City of Refuge! God gave me a place of safety where the people didn't judge me, and they showed me what pure love looks like.

## Your truth matters

Your truth and reality is not others truth and reality. It does not mean that the abuse, or situation did not happen. It just means that the person does not see it in your point of view. Speak your truth regardless of what others may think. When you speak your truth, it sets you free. Yes, speaking your truth is scary! However, the City taught me that, "If you don't come out of your comfort zone, then you won't grow".

## Seek help

Seeking help does not mean you are weak. I was looking for hope. I was searching for peace! I went to friends, teachers, counselors upon counselors, to a

# The City of Refuge Changed Our Lives

variety of church leaders, until I found one that knew what was going on with me and was willing to work with me to overcome my issues. I found the City of Refuge: the place that didn't make me feel like a statistic. I was crazy or like I was a problem or underclass citizen. At the City, I found God, but I gained the practical life skills and techniques that honestly kept me alive.

Author Anika Stewart says, "Have your moment but don't stay there". She also says, "I CHOOSE to L.I.V.E". What is your choice today? You have the same choices that I had to make. "If you want change, you have to change your perspective (Stewart, 2018). It is about your action! My hope is that if you are dealing with mental health, seek God! God will give you clear instructions! Trust yourself, and value who you are! You get one life to live! Choose to live life to the fullest!

# The City of Refuge Changed Our Lives

The City of Refuge Changed Our Lives

# From Lost Boy to Beloved Husband
# Isaiah M. Kilgo-Felder

Pastor and Founder of Music Empire

# The City of Refuge Changed Our Lives

The City of Refuge Changed Our Lives

# From Lost Boy to Beloved Husband

Isaiah M. Kilgo-Felder, Business Professional and Youth Activist; with Degrees in Christian Ministry and Christian Education. At the age of twenty-two years old he has become a Pastor at The City of Refuge Inc. in 2016. He has served under the tutelage of Apostle Dr. Ira D. Roach III.

With certifications in School age Education and Development, and Mental Health Studies, he has progressed and earned a certification as a life coach. Isaiah is also the founder of the Music Empire where he teaches students the gift of music and is the founder of the "Millennial Movement." Isaiah is passionate about helping others in need and is a trailblazer for the millennials.

My journey began August 15th, 2014 I came to the City of Refuge. I had just dropped out of high school and I was really playing with my life at the time. I was not part of a church at the time. I was just going to churches and playing for them. If they needed me to preach I would. I did not know the true value of ministry or being committed to one. So, I came to the City and I thought they were just like every other church. With time, I later found that thought to be wrong.

The City of Refuge showed me so much love and compassion. It felt weird because I had never had that type of experience before when it came to people because I didn't trust people. But it was something about the City. I was accustomed to being called a "liar" and "you are bad and you are always in trouble". I carried that with me all to find out that they never labeled me they encouraged and uplifted me. The City of Refuge let me see a different side of life. I remember later in the month of September I was having a conversation with Dr. Roach and he was talking to me about being a man and he said something that stuck with me forever. He said, "Isaiah I don't need your gifts I need you to become a man". At that time being 18 and no active father and being on my own I did not understand what that meant until later on down the road.

In September 2014, I started going back to school and I was working at the Music School of Delaware. I became an active member at The City of Refuge and my life began to change. I began to learn about personal development and how to take personal responsibility. I began to learn things about how to do action plans, understanding the mindset: these were things that I had never heard or learned in church before. Yes, they had church, but it was different. I learned how to convert my gift into a stream of income. I found my niche in teaching and working with the youth. Being at The City of Refuge, I learned how to love, how to take self-evaluation and personal correction.

In June of 2015, I graduated from High School and I

## The City of Refuge Changed Our Lives

was student of the year. This was one of the greatest days in my life. The City of Refuge was there to support me. My journey had its ups and downs, but I can say that though it all, The City of Refuge has never turned its back on me. It has pushed me in the direction of my purpose and my destiny. In 2016, I had my first child. This was in the midst of trying to figure out what I wanted to do with my life. Battling with who I was and knowing my purpose, I felt lost but the City of Refuge pushed me through the testing times. They sat down with me and regardless of the outside chatter and opinions of people, they taught me how to love and helped me understand.

Yes, I may have fallen but that does not mean that destiny and purpose for my life has ended. So, I picked myself up and I began to mature and learn more. I became the Youth Program Director for the City of Refuge and I gained employment with the Boys and Girls Club of America. Through the prayers and encouragement of my church, God granted me extreme favor. Being at The City, I have become a certified life coach and obtained several degrees in ministry. I am a father of two children and I am getting ready to become a husband.

The City of Refuge has changed my life tremendously. They have taught me things that I never knew and things I thought I knew I had to relearn. They taught me the value of manhood and the cycles that I had in my life stopped some of the struggles that I dealt with. I was never judged, never talked about, and never criticized. I was always treated with love and compassion. I was always given honest and great counsel and wisdom. I could not ask for a better church and family than The City of Refuge. They really help people recover from hurts, habits and hang-ups. I am grateful that I was one of the people they helped. It is not easy accepting help from people when you are used to doing things by yourself.

The most valuable principal the City of Refuge taught me is teamwork. I was so accustomed to doing things on my own. I had to really understand that things do not get done with one person. I understood that things get done with a team. It was hard for me to learn but I got it. I learned to open up more at the City of Refuge. I learned to share my problems and how I was feeling. I was able to depend on people who, when they say they have your back, they really have your back. I never had to second guess myself when it came to my City of Refuge family because what you saw is what you Got.

Coming to The City of Refuge for me was not a choice but part of the journey God has for me and my family. So, did it change my life? Well it did something way beyond that it gave me a chance at life, a chance at purpose, and a chance at destiny. The City of Refuge created opportunities for me to reach my highest potential and most of all it released the King in me. It has helped me to find out who I

## The City of Refuge Changed Our Lives

am, what I possess, unlocked my creativity, and gave me hope. Through my struggles and setbacks, I still have a destiny and I still have a purpose. Thank you, City of Refuge for turning this lost boy into mature, God fearing, father, leader and husband.

# The City of Refuge Changed Our Lives

The City of Refuge Changed Our Lives

# Overcoming Emotional Abuse
# Dr. Darrell M. Canady

Minister

# The City of Refuge Changed Our Lives

The City of Refuge Changed Our Lives

# Overcoming Emotional Abuse

For two decades, I served in various Christian ministries on the East Coast. These ministries consisted of Methodist, Pentecostal, and Deliverance. Each ministry provided me with different experiences, where I either grew or I was emotionally harmed. The harm came in the form of emotional abuse. As a result, I was crippled by confusion, anger, hurt, depression, and instability. Certain ministries wreaked havoc on my psyche because I was left feeling ostracized, misunderstood, under-anointed, and fake. The pastors and/or members would either suggest to me that I was a homosexual, an outcast, or not capable of preaching or ministering God's word effectively. I was hurt and crushed for many years. Thus, I developed a pattern of "backsliding" and "church hopping." I was merely attempting to find a church home that truly accepted me and would not emotionally abuse me.

In the late 2000's, I became affiliated with The City of Refuge Church, Inc., where the overseer is Apostle, Dr. Ira D. Roach III. Under Apostle Roach's guidance and nurturing, I began to learn that I indeed had a voice, and I was "somebody" in ministry. The City of Refuge Church never judged me, never once abandoned me, and always lifted me up when I was at my lowest point in my life. Previous ministries did not always do this. I was stolen from; talked about; betrayed; called names (i.e., faggot, gay, etc.); and chastised for befriending other effeminate males in the church. Therefore, I took it upon myself to learn more about how "emotional abuse" impacted my life through scholarly and biblical research.

## The nature of emotional abuse

Feeling insulted and wounded. Never measuring up. Walking on eggshells (Gordon, 2018). If these statements describe your relationship(s), it is likely you are being emotionally abused (Gordon, 2018). In general, a relationship(s) is emotionally abusive when there is a consistent pattern of abusive words and bullying behaviors that wear down a person's self-esteem and undermine their mental health (Gordon, 2018). What is more, mental or emotional abuse, while most common in dating and married relationships, can occur in any relationship including among friends, family members, and co-workers (Gordon, 2018).

According to Gordon (2018), emotional abuse is one of the hardest forms of abuse to recognize. It can be subtle and insidious or overt and manipulative. Either way, it chips away at the victim's self-esteem and they begin to doubt their perceptions and reality (Gordon, 2018). The underlying goal in emotional abuse is to control the victim by discrediting, isolating, and silencing (Gordon, 2018). In the end, the victim feels trapped (Gordon, 2018). They are often too wounded to endure the relationship any longer, but also too afraid to leave (Gordon, 2018). So the cycle just repeats itself until something is done (Gordon, 2018).

According to Gordon (2018), when emotional abuse is severe and ongoing, a victim may lose their entire sense of self, sometimes without a single mark or bruise. Instead, the wounds are invisible to others, hidden in the self-doubt, worthlessness and self-loathing the victim feels (Gordon, 2018). In fact, says Gordon, many victims say that the scars from emotional abuse last far longer and are much deeper than those from physical abuse. Over time, the accusations, verbal abuse, name-calling, criticisms, and gas-lighting erode a victim's sense of self so much that they can no longer see themselves realistically (Gordon, 2018). Consequently, states Gordon, the victim begins to agree with the abuser and becomes internally critical. Once this happens, most victims become trapped…believing that they will never be good enough… (Gordon, 2018).

## Overcoming emotional abuse

In order for one to overcome emotional abuse, one needs to develop three (3) critical "Plans of Action" followed with biblical scripture to increase their self-confidence while serving in a "perceived" abusive ministry.

Firstly, one needs to identify and face the emotional abuse for exactly what it is. With physical pain, according to Udodiong, you can see where it hurts so you know where the bandage is needed. With emotional pain, you can't see it so you might not know what to do or where to start from with the healing process. Thus, it is sometimes necessary to turn to God, He knows everything including how to heal you (Udodiong, 2018). According to Udodiong, His words provide comfort and give you the strength to move on. In his letter, St Peter writes, "And after you have suffered a little while, the God of all grace, who has called you to his eternal glory in Christ, will himself restore, confirm, strengthen, and establish you" (1 Peter 5:10). Truly, as the Psalmist says, "He healeth the broken in heart, and bindeth up their wounds" (Psalms 147:3).

Secondly, in order to overcome emotional abuse one needs to pray. Pray before confronting your perceived abuser. It is hard to confront an abusive person especially when it is…not easily banished (Hammond, 2017). The abuse may be mild but nonetheless is hurtful and harmful in several ways (Hammond, 2017). According to Hammond, here are some suggestions for handling abusive people:

- ✓ ***See it.*** Begin to see the different types of abuse for what they are. At the beginning, this is done long after the abuse has occurred. Eventually, awareness can happen while it is occurring.
- ✓ ***Speak it.*** This step requires quite a bit of courage and strength. It first begins by having

the victim speak the type of abuse tactic being used in their mind. Repeat this exercise over and over to gain the necessary bravery before addressing an abuser. This is not a harsh speak (there is no benefit to be gaining by being just as abusive as an abuser), rather it is a soft approach. The intent is to bring awareness to the abuser that they are being abusive and allow them to back off or save face.

✓ **Stress it.** If the abuser continues to shatter boundaries, the victim needs to begin by saying, "I'm not going to take this anymore." Now is the time to add more weight to the statements by letting the abuser know there are consequences for violating personal boundaries. Of course, this means the victim must be aware of their own boundaries first.

✓ **Stand by it.** Once a consequence has been stated, it must be carried out if the abuse continues. Otherwise, the abuser will just intensify the abuse next time. It is important to have someone hold the victim accountable for their boundary setting and enforcement. It is clear from the Bible that we are meant to live in peace and be happy. John 14:27 states that, 'Peace I leave with you, my peace I give unto you: not as the world giveth, give I unto you. Let not your heart be troubled, neither let it be afraid'. In effect, The LORD shall fight for you, and ye shall hold your peace

(Exodus 14:14). This gives the much needed support when the victim is again being attacked by the abuser.

Third and last way to overcome emotional abuse is to control of your life. While all abuse involves issues of power and control, emotional abuse gets underneath a victim's skin and makes them second guess themselves (Break the Cycle, 2014). Remember, this is all based on control, says Break the Cycle. An abuser wants to feel good about themselves, so they may project their own feelings of powerlessness...or try to ensure they are never rejected themselves (Break the Cycle, 2014). But those feelings are their feelings and are not necessarily rooted in truth (Break the Cycle, 2014). So how can someone in an emotionally abusive relationship take control back? According to Break the Cycle (2014), there is need to set boundaries with their partner and explain how they are open to hearing concerns. They need to consider personal values, desires, and needs when discussing what can and cannot be done (Break the Cycle, 2014). If they cannot meet these reasonable expectations, states Break the Cycle, then it's time to move on for 'Many [are] the afflictions of the righteous: but the LORD delivereth him out of them all' (Psalms 34:19).

In conclusion, the only way abuse stops is for people to stand up to it (Hammond, 2017). While this is difficult, it is not impossible. It is possible to have a relationship that is free from abusive behavior

# The City of Refuge Changed Our Lives

(Hammond, 2017). Reaching out to someone who can offer support will help in the long run, as they can be there during this difficult time (Break the Cycle, 2014). They can also help victims remember what it used to be like before the relationship, and how they are worthy and lovable (Break the Cycle, 2014). At the end of the day, states Break the Cycle, love is not controlling. It's not about trying to change a person, but rather about celebrating that person (Break the Cycle, 2014). Everyone deserves a healthy relationship and I found this at The City of Refuge.

References

Break the Cycle. (2014). Leaving an Emotionally Abusive Relationship. Retrieved from the World Wide Web on September 15, 2018.

Gordon, S. (2018). How to Identify and Cope with Emotional Abuse. Retrieved from the World Wide Web at: www.verywellmind.com on September 15, 2018.

Hammond, C. (2017). How to Confront an Abusive Person. Retrieved from the World Wide Web at: https://pro.psychcentral.com on September 15, 2018.

Udodiong, I. (2017). 10 Bible Verses for Dealing with Emotional Pain. Retrieved from the World Wide Web at: www.pulse.ng on September 15, 2018.

# The City of Refuge Changed Our Lives

## About the Author

Born in a small village in Uganda, Dr Patrick Businge did not let his circumstances characterized by war and abject poverty become his standard. Following his dreams while believing that no condition was permanent, he took steps to raise above his circumstances and made greatness his benchmark.

Dr Patrick Businge has gone on to become the Founder of Greatness University: the world's first institution dedicated to discovering, unlocking, and monetising greatness in individuals and businesses. His main goal is to help you tap into your greatness faster and easily than you can ever imagine.

# The City of Refuge Changed Our Lives

Dr Patrick Businge is an educator. He has taught over 50,000 people in classrooms, churches, orphanages, villages, community centres, and boardrooms throughout the United Kingdom of Great Britain, Europe, Africa, and the Americas.

Dr Patrick Businge is also a strong believer in lifelong learning and personal development. He has studied in over 7 universities and acquired over 10 postgraduate qualifications. He has researched, written and spoken for approximately 20 years in the fields of ethics, philosophy, religion, education, armed conflict, disability, and greatness. Living in a world characterised by war, plagued by a shortage of hope and marred with average performance, his ultimate vision is to inspire one million people become instruments of peace, messengers of hope and channels of greatness. It is because of his vision and insight that he has recently got an Authentic Leadership Award.

Dr Patrick Businge is a bestselling author. He has written various books including:
- 7 Steps to Greatness: The **Masterplan** to Take Your Life, Studies, Career and Business to the Next Level
- Les Brown Changed Our Lives: 77 Stories to Inspire You to Live Your Dreams
- The Road to Your Best Self: Discover Your Miracle Power, Uncommon Nature and the Greatness in You

# The City of Refuge Changed Our Lives

He is a Book Creation Coach and Celebrity Researcher. He runs retreats on how to discover, write, publish, and monetise the book in you.

Dr Patrick Businge speaks to various audiences on Personal and Professional Development. His exciting talks, transformational seminars and life changing boot camps on *7 Steps to Greatness, Book Writing, STAR Goals, Success Mindset, and Finding Your Best Self* bring about immediate change and long-term results.

Dr Patrick Businge has travelled and worked in over 10 countries on 3 continents. He speaks four languages: English, French, Swahili and some Arabic. Patrick is happily married and has 2 children. He is active in community and national affairs. To learn more about his programs, seminars and services, please visit **www.greatness-university.com**. If you have any personal questions email him directly at info@greatness-university.com or meet him on Facebook, LinkedIn and Instagram.

# The City of Refuge Changed Our Lives